Space Explorer

THE STARS

Patricia Whitehouse

Heinemann Library
Chicago, Illinois

© 2004 Heinemann Library
a division of Reed Elsevier Inc.
Chicago, Illinois
Customer Service 888-454-2279

Visit our website at www.heinemannlibrary.com

Designed by Heinemann Library
Printed in China by South China Printing.

08 07 06 05 04

10 9 8 7 6 5 4 3 2 1

Library of Congress Cataloging-in-Publication Data

Whitehouse, Patricia, 1958-
  Stars / Patricia Whitehouse.
      v. cm. -- (Space explorer)

  Includes bibliographical references and index.
  Contents: What are stars? -- The sun, our closest star -- The Milky Way -- Other galaxies -- Star nurseries -- Star energy -- Star color and temperature -- Star sizes -- Big explosions -- Twinkling stars -- Changing night sky -- Sky pictures -- A constellation story -- Amazing sun facts.

  ISBN 1-4034-5156-7 (lib. bdg.) -- ISBN 1-4034-5660-7 (pbk.)

  1. Stars--Juvenile literature. [1. Stars.] I. Title. II. Series.

  QB801.7.W45 2004

  523.8--dc22

                        2003026767

Acknowledgments
The author and publishers are grateful to the following for permission to reproduce copyright material:

Cover photograph: H.Richer/NASA

pp. 4–5 Corbis (royalty free); p. 6 Corbis (royalty free); p. 7 David Malin/UK Schmidt Telescope; p. 8 Science Photo Library; p. 9 David Talent/NOAO; p. 10 Chuck Claver, Nigel Sharp/NOAO; p. 11 C. Sarazin et al./NASA; p. 12 Nathan Smith/NOAO; p. 13 Science Photo Library; p. 14 Corbis (royalty free); p. 15 Space Telescope Science Institute, NASA/Science Photo Library; p. 16 European Southern Observatory/Science Photo Library; p. 17 Science Photo Library; p. 18 Mark Garlick/Science Photo Library; p. 20 J-C Cuillandre/Science Photo Library; p. 21 Chandra X-Ray Observatory, NASA/Science Photo Library; p. 22 Roger Ressmeyer/Corbis; p. 23 NASA; p. 24 Science Photo Library; p. 25 Danny Lehman/Corbis; p. 26 Jerry Schad/Science Photo Library; p. 27 Eckhard Slawik/Science Photo Library; p. 28 Francis Diego; p. 29 Frank Zullo/Science Photo Library

Every effort has been made to contact copyright holders of any material reproduced in this book. Any omissions will be rectified in subsequent printings if notice is given to the publisher.

Special thanks to Geza Gyuk of the Adler Planetarium for his comments in preparation of this book.

Some words are shown in bold, **like this.** You can find out what they mean by looking in the glossary.

Contents

The night sky is full of stars. Each star looks like a tiny point of light. But stars are not really small.

They are huge balls of hot **gases.** They look small because they are so far away from Earth.

The Sun is a star. It is the closest star to Earth, but it is 93 million miles (150 million kilometers) away.

The next closest star to the Earth is called Proxima Centauri. It is 265,000 times farther away from the Earth than the Sun.

If you could drive a car to the Sun, it would take 173 years to get there. But it would take over 46 million years to drive to the next closest star!

The Milky Way

A **galaxy** is a huge group of stars. The Sun and many other stars we see are part of a huge group of stars called the Milky Way galaxy.

There are over 200 billion stars in the Milky Way.

8

On a clear, dark night, part of the Milky Way can be seen in the sky. The stars are so close together that they look like a milky-white band across the sky.

Other Galaxies

There are billions of **galaxies.** Most galaxies are very far away from Earth and can only be seen with a telescope.

Each of these bright spots is a galaxy containing billions of stars.

galaxy

This galaxy is round and flat, unlike the Milky Way.

Galaxies have many different shapes. The Milky Way is called a spiral galaxy because it has a flat, spiral shape. Some galaxies are round. Other galaxies have no real shape at all.

11

Stars begin as huge clouds of **gas** in space. The gas squeezes together and gets very hot. The squeezed gas begins to glow and a star is born.

It takes millions of years for a new star to be made.

12

The bright spots are the new stars made in this nebula, called the Eagle nebula.

A cloud of gas in space is called a **nebula.** A special telescope is needed to see the nebula and the new stars inside.

Star Energy

In the middle of stars, **gas** is squeezed together so much that tiny parts of different gases join up. This makes powerful **nuclear energy.** Nuclear energy makes the stars hot and bright.

This group of stars is about 40 million years old.

Stars give out a lot of nuclear energy. In one second, a star like the Sun gives out as much energy as people would use in a million years.

People use nuclear energy from power plants to make heat and electricity on Earth.

Star Colors

Not all stars are yellow like the Sun. Stars can be blue, white, or red, too. A star's color depends on its **temperature**.

The bright stars are young, red stars.

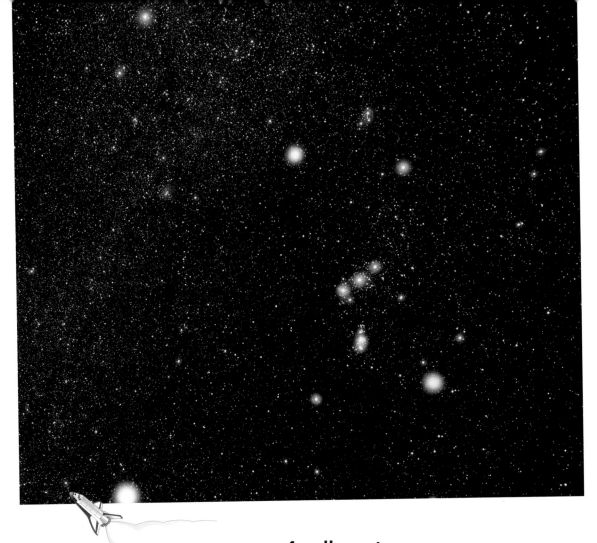

The outer parts of yellow stars can get as hot as 11,000 °F (6000 °C).

Blue stars are the hottest. The next hottest are white stars, and then yellow stars. The Sun is a yellow star. Stars with the lowest temperature are red.

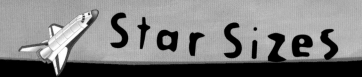

Star Sizes

Sirius B

Earth

Over one million Earths could fit inside the Sun, but the Sun is not the biggest star. Red giants and supergiants are the largest stars. **White dwarfs** are small, hot stars.

18

Proxima Centauri

Sun

Sirius B is a white dwarf and Proxima Centauri is a red dwarf. They are both smaller than the Sun.

After billions of years, stars use up their energy and change. Some smaller stars lose some of their **gases** and then become **white dwarfs.**

The gases from a dying small star join together to make nebulae. This is where new stars may form.

This is what was left
after a supernova.
The explosion
was not big
enough to make
a black hole.

Big stars explode. These huge
explosions are called **supernovae.**
A black hole might be all that is left
after an explosion. In black holes
gravity is so strong that not even
light can escape.

# Twinkling Stars

Stars are round, like the Sun. But they do not seem round if you look at them from the Earth. They look like twinkling points of light.

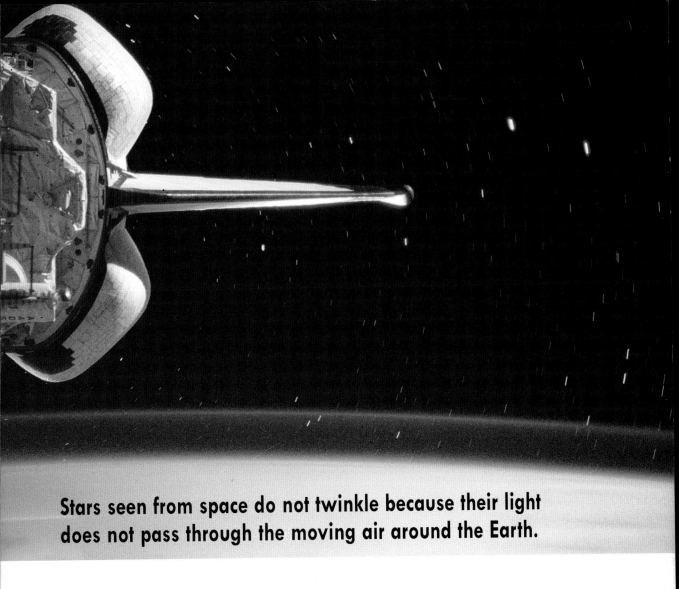

Stars seen from space do not twinkle because their light does not pass through the moving air around the Earth.

Stars twinkle because when we look at them we see their light through the moving air that is around the Earth. The moving air makes the starlight wiggle so it looks like the stars are twinkling.

Changing Night Sky

Long ago, people noticed that the stars in the sky changed place during the year. They also noticed that the stars came back to the same place at the same time every year.

People learned to use stars to figure out the time. In South America, the stars showed the Maya people when it was time to plant crops.

This is the ruins of an observatory the Maya people used in Mexico.

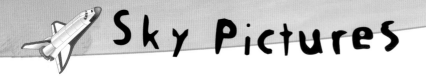

Sky Pictures

People began to see shapes in groups of stars. They named the shapes and told stories to try to explain how the shapes were made.

This group of stars is called the Plow. Lines have been added to show its shape.

This group of stars makes a W shape. It is called Cassiopeia.

A group of stars that form a shape is called a **constellation.** Many constellations were named by the Ancient Greeks. Other cultures also had stories about constellations.

A Constellation Story

Orion is a **constellation** that looks like a man hunting. Some stars form a belt along the hunter's waist. A hunting knife hangs from the belt.

Lines have been added to show Orion's shape. Can you see his belt?

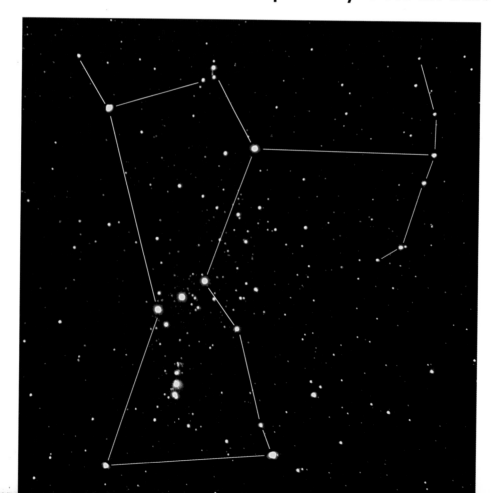

There is an ancient story from Greece about Orion the hunter. He was in love with a goddess named Diana, but Orion died before they could marry. Diana put him in the sky as a group of stars to remember him.

This group of stars is named Scorpio, after the scorpion that was supposed to have killed Orion.

Amazing Star Facts

- Stars can last for billions of years.

- Scientists think there might be hundreds of billions of **galaxies** in the **universe.** Each galaxy may have billions of stars.

- A **red giant** is 30 times bigger than the Sun.

- A brown dwarf is the smallest type of star.

Glossary

constellation group of stars that make a shape

galaxy group of gases, dust, and billions of stars

gas airlike material that is not solid or liquid

gravity force that pulls objects together

nebula cloud of gas in space, where stars are made

nuclear energy when different parts of a gas join together to make powerful energy

red dwarf small star with a cool temperature

red giant huge star with a temperature lower than that of other stars

supernova the explosion of a very large star

white dwarf small star with a high temperature

More Books to Read

Whitehouse, Patricia. *The Sun (Space Explorer)*. Chicago: Heinemann Library, 2004.

Index